Book Summary
of the Key Points
in

Kerry Patterson, Joseph Grenny,
Ron McMillan, and Al Switzler

Crucial Conversations
Tools for Talking
When Stakes Are High

by Executive Reads

Welcome to this Executive Reads summary of Crucial Conversations by Kerry Patterson, Joseph Grenny, Ron McMillan, and Al Switzler. This summary is a production of Kronos Books, produced by the Executive Reads writing team, edited by Richard Finn.

This summary is meant to provide insight into the Crucial Conversations book, if you are considering reading it - or providing you with a refresher of the concepts contained therein, if you already read it.

Executive Reads (2015-11-05). Book Summary of Crucial Conversations Tools for Talking When Stakes Are High - Key Points Summary/Refresher with Crib Sheet Infographic. Executive Reads. Kindle Edition.

Introduction

The effects of conversations on our lives cannot be understated. How people see us, respond to our directions, and make decisions affecting us mostly depend on our conversations. We often need to take part in productive conversations about important and sensitive topics, even if we didn't realize it when the conversation began. Many people lack the skills and preparation to conduct those conversations in an inclusive and respectful way. The acclaimed business book *Crucial Conversations* by authors Kerry Patterson, Joseph Grenny, Ron McMillan, and Al Switzler sheds light on identifying and navigating the conversations that mark the difference between success and failure.

Conversations form an important part of daily life, and as such, some people may overlook them as a cause of problems in the workplace or at home. Talking to co-workers and subordinates requires first understanding what turns a conversation from mundane to crucial, and second, knowing how to handle that conversation in a way that produces the desired result. Conducting a crucial conversation skillfully can turn a disgruntled employee into a satisfied one, and a failed product into a success. *Crucial Conversations* serves as a guide to help people identify crucial conversations as they happen.

The book shows how, once a conversation becomes crucial, participants can eliminate common pitfalls and problems to ensure the dialogue remains safe for all parties and focuses on the most critical issues at hand. Creating safety and building a mutual purpose turn a dialogue full of potential difficulties into a beneficial conversation for all parties concerned.

After demonstrating how to steer a crucial conversation out of the danger zone, the book shows specific techniques that allow managers and workers to navigate tricky topics with confidence. Sharing information and using the tools provided in the book, people from every walk of life can learn to approach crucial conversations knowing they can avoid the mistakes that sink negotiations and lead to a breakdown of communications.

Executive Reads Rating

Important Concepts

Crucial Conversation: Any conversation that meets one or more of these criteria: the opinions of the participants vary, the stakes are high, and the emotions of participants are also heightened. Typically, the results of the conversation may make a big impact on some aspect of the participants' lives.

The Fool's Choice: The false options that many people believe form their only choices in a crucial conversation: to speak up and make enemies, or to suffer in silence while others make bad decisions.

Pool of Shared Meaning: The information shared by all participants in a crucial conversation. Every participant must contribute relevant histories, opinions and facts to the pool.

Mutual Purpose: A common goal or desire agreed upon by every participant in a crucial conversation.

CRIB: A technique to create mutual purpose consisting of four steps:
1. Commit to finding a mutual purpose
2. Recognize the reason behind the behaviors

3. Invent a mutual purpose
4. Brainstorm new strategies to achieve each other's purpose

STATE: An acronym representing the skills required to conduct a crucial conversation about any sensitive topic:
1. Share the facts
2. Tell your story
3. Ask for others' paths
4. Talk tentatively
5. Encourage testing

AMPP: An acronym that stands for four valuable listening skills that can make it safe for participants in a conversation to speak honestly:
1. Ask questions to get the ball rolling
2. Mirror to confirm the speaker's feelings
3. Paraphrase the speaker's story in your own words
4. Prime the pool by offering an educated guess about the speaker's problem

Path to Action: The conversational roadmap that illustrates each participant's primary concerns in a dialogue.

Chapter 1
What Makes a Conversation Crucial?

What is a crucial conversation, and why does it matter? People who possess strong communications skills – those who can navigate difficult topics with ease – achieve great success more often than people who stumble when called upon to discuss sensitive or emotional issues. Crucial conversations – conversations that have the potential to make a big difference in some aspect of life – happen every day. They occur in the workplace between co-workers as well as between management and subordinates. They happen at home among family members and socially among friends. The ability to step into such conversations with confidence lies at the heart of success, both professionally and personally.

A crucial conversation may start out as crucial, but at times even the most mundane conversation can become crucial as it happens. A crucial conversation is one in which:

1. The opinions of participants about a given situation vary, sometimes dramatically.
2. The stakes riding on the outcome of the conversation are high, with the potential to have a

significant impact on the participants' lives.

3. Emotions among the participants in the conversation become heightened, making the conversation itself feel like a minefield.

Any conversation in any area of life has the potential to be crucial.

Many people lack the skills to conduct a crucial conversation in a safe and productive way. On the surface the options for holding a crucial conversation seem simple:

1. Avoid the conversation entirely.
2. Handle the conversation poorly.
3. Handle the conversation well.

Everyone wants to handling the conversation, yet doing so presents some serious challenges. To begin with, people are not biologically equipped to handle stress equitably. The human body releases a host of chemicals in stressful situations, triggering the well known "fight or flight" response. When the "fight or flight" response activates, the body takes energy away from what it considers to be non-essential functions to provide additional power to things like the ability to run or fight. Unfortunately, one of the abilities that loses energy in stressful situations is the ability to think clearly at a high level.

The addition of pressure represents a complication. Unfortunately, crucial conversations rarely advertise themselves in advance. A seemingly normal talk always has a chance to transform into a crucial one with little or no warning. When that occurs the people involved often lack preparation and it increases the chances that the "fight or flight" response will kick in.

Crucial conversations stump us. Few people possess a natural ability to conduct crucial conversations with ease. Societally speaking, people lack good role models for how to discuss charged topics. The lack of available examples complicates dialogue because the participants know they must act as trailblazers if they want to be successful.

Finally, many people behave in ways that undermine their good intentions in a crucial conversation. For example, they resort to sarcasm when they are upset, or they release frustration by complaining about others behind their backs. Sometimes instead of initiating a productive conversation they might choose to nag or nitpick. When the time for the crucial conversation arrives, the participants must overcome a history of bad blood and hurt feelings if they want to accomplish anything.

Some examples of crucial conversations include ending a relationship, critiquing a co-worker's project, speaking to a boss who breaks his own rules, dealing with a rebellious child, or giving an unfavorable performance review.

The Law of Crucial Conversations says that the ability to talk effectively about emotionally or politically sensitive topics is the key leadership skill that all great leaders must possess. Crucial conversations loom large in every aspect of life. Many people choose silence over having a crucial conversation, but research shows that silence costs money, sinks companies, and ruins lives.

Just as avoiding crucial conversations can lead to disastrous results, embracing them has some significant benefits, including career advancement, improved relationships, improved organizations, and better personal health. No successful person got that way by staying silent and avoiding crucial conversations.

Chapter 2
The Power of Dialogue

Few people possess the skills necessary to handle crucial conversations in the right way. As a rule, they approach any critical dialogue with a set of false assumptions – things that leave them feeling nervous, stressed, and unwilling to shoulder the burden of raising a controversial or emotional topic. In *Crucial Conversations*, the authors refer to these false assumptions as The Fool's Choice.

The participants in crucial conversations may resort to defensive tactics. They play games, sink into silence, or react in an emotional or self-defeating way. The tactics all act as a form of sabotage – unintentional, but harmful nevertheless. People turn to defensive tactics as a way of shielding themselves from discomfort. They sense that the conversation has become critical, and they fall victim to The Fool's Choice.

The Fool's Choice presents participants in a crucial conversation with a false set of options. They believe that the only way to emerge from a difficult conversation intact requires one of two potential responses:

1.   Speaking up about emotional or risky topics and turning the other participants in the conversation

into enemies; or

2. Remaining silent, essentially voting for whatever result the other participants in the conversation choose.

The Fool's Choice makes people feel as though they must choose between candor and kindness. Many people learn this lesson early in life. They can point to a time when they were honest without care for another person's emotions, and remember in great detail the hurt and misunderstanding their unfiltered honesty caused. They grow up believing that honesty and cruelty go hand in hand.

A person who possesses the skills to navigate crucial conversations understands that The Fool's Choice is a false one. Instead of assuming that the above options exist in a vacuum, the skilled conversationalist sees a third option: to bring up emotionally charged or risky topics in a way that brings the participants together instead of turning them into enemies. He or she discusses difficult subjects in a way that respects the other people in the room and gives them space to offer their own opinions and emotions.

Conducting a crucial conversation, then, requires that at least one participant refuses The Fool's Choice and takes the lead in navigating through the risky parts of the conversation. This step allows for dialogue, which the dictionary defines as "the free flow of meaning between two or more people."

"Meaning" represents a key departure from the way many of us think about dialogue. Many people define dialogue as the flow of words, but different words can mean different things to different people. For that reason, a crucial conversation requires that the participants contribute to the Pool of Shared Meaning.

The Pool of Shared Meaning describes the information shared by all participants in a crucial conversation. Each person in the conversation brings to it their own opinions, feelings, experiences, and thoughts about the topic of the conversation. An individual's perception of the conversation is their personal pool of meaning, but the only way to guarantee that the other participants understand that perception is by voicing it – adding it to the pool of common knowledge, or the Pool of Shared Meaning to use the book's term. In a crucial conversation, some participants may hesitate to speak their minds. For the Pool of Shared Meaning to be helpful, though, it must contain contributions from every person in the room. Without it, the collective IQ of the people involved in the conversation decreases and the likelihood of misunderstandings increases.

When the Pool of Shared Meaning lacks contributions from all participants, dialogue suffers. The participants in the conversation become less intelligent because they do not possess key information. This ignorance leads to game playing. Two major games have the potential to kill dialogue before it starts:

- Freeze Your Lover. When dialogue breaks down, some people give the other participant(s) the cold shoulder hoping to achieve the desired result. This very rarely works because the other person ends up feeling rejected and shut off. Freezing your lover can also include aggressive tactics such as using sarcasm, humor, innuendo, and even facial expressions to express displeasure with the situation.

- Salute and Stay Mute. A variation on Freeze Your Lover, Salute and Stay Mute rears its head in work situations when subordinates go along with what their leader decides and keep their dissenting opinions and dissatisfaction to themselves.

Dialogue skills may not come easily to everybody, but they are something that people can learn at any point in life. The remainder of the book talks about specific tools people can use to successfully handle crucial conversations as they arise.

Chapter 3
Start with Heart

Creating the opportunity for productive dialogue requires at least one participant in the conversation to take the initiative. If all parties lack the ability to look within and take responsibility for their own part in an existing problem, the possibility of resolution shrinks. In order to create a safe space for dialogue, one or more of the people involved must understand the need to start with heart.

Starting with Yourself

Every person, at one time or another, has discovered that they are part of the problem instead of part of the solution. The reason that so many crucial conversations go awry is the inability of some people to accept responsibility for their own actions. The people who find the most success negotiating crucial conversations have the willingness and insight to acknowledge their own problems first and foremost.

Masters of crucial conversation understand that they lack the wherewithal to control the thoughts, actions, and behavior of the other people in the room. They recognize that they control their own thoughts and behavior, and they embrace that responsibility fully. Because they do so, they strive continuously to improve their conversational skills.

The key to crucial conversation lies in the heart. A skilled conversationalist recognizes the moment that a conversation becomes crucial. Instead of lashing out or plunging ahead without thought, he stops to evaluate his own feelings and desires. This pause allows him to navigate the conversation with skill and finesse because he understands what he wants and why he wants it.

Identifying Goals

When a conversation turns crucial, emotions run high. In an emotionally volatile situation, participants sometimes allow their true goals – the ones that really matter – to disappear. Often that means that a person's goal changes when the conversation shifts. These three goals most commonly displace the important goals:

- The need to win. When a participant in a crucial conversation receives a challenge or criticism, his real goal may get lost because he feels a strong desire to "win" the conversation by proving the person who challenged him wrong. He wants to correct errors and mistaken perceptions, and he loses sight of the goal he intended to achieve before the conversation took a turn.
- The need to dole out punishment. When one party to a conversation introduces inflammatory or sensitive data into the Pool of Shared Information, the person whom the information most affects may feel the desire to punish the person who poisoned the pool. While punishment might feel necessary

and righteous, it does nothing to further the conversation or resolve the issues at hand.

- The need to keep the peace. Sometimes the result of a conversation becoming crucial takes a more passive turn. Depending upon the personality of the person most affected by the conversation, the possibility exists that, instead of winning or punishment, a desire to keep the peace takes over the conversation. While on the surface this goal might seem preferable to discord, it produces results that fail to solve the real problem.

Fortunately, a skilled person, with effort, can avoid all of the false goals above and refocus the conversation by doing the following:

1. Identify the true goal. Before responding to critical information or accusations, a skilled conversationalist pauses and reconnects with her initial goal. She remembers what she wants to achieve and refuses the Fool's Choice. She asks herself, "What do I really want here?" and she answers that question honestly.

2. She refocuses her brain on her true goal and thinks about what she can do to achieve it. She asks himself questions that allow her to move back into dialogue.

3. She takes control of her body by asking complex questions that move the brain from "fight or flight" mode and prepare it for rational thought.

Searching for 'And'

After the skilled conversationalist has reminded himself of his true goals, refocused his brain, and claimed control of his body, he takes another critical step that ensures the success of a crucial conversation. Many crucial conversations hang on either/or situations. The parties involved feel that they must decide between two competing outcomes. The skilled conversationalist helps all parties look for 'And.'

Looking for 'And' involves convincing all parties that common goals exist. Discovering common goals present a challenge, but a patient and willing person takes a few easy steps to align the people involved behind a common goal:

1. Clarify what he really wants. In a crucial conversation, people sometimes make assumptions about what others want. The only way to ensure that this doesn't happen is to articulate, clearly and in no uncertain terms, the desired goal.

2. Clarify what he doesn't want. While expressing a desired goal helps avoid confusion, articulating the worst-case scenario has its benefits too – especially if all of the involved parties find that scenario distasteful.

3. Ask a question that combines the two. Asking a more complex question puts the brain into logical mode. It forces everybody involved to take a step back and consider the possibility of 'And' – and it invites calm, rational conversation.

In order for the above steps to work, the parties in the

conversation must accept the possibility of discussing difficult topics without creating enemies. If that mindset doesn't exist, the involved parties may end up getting stuck, and the crucial conversation can turn into a disaster.

Chapter 4
Creating Safety

Crucial conversations consist of two primary ingredients: content and conditions. The things people say, as well as the Pool of Shared Information, make up the content of the conversation. It can be a little harder to pin down the conditions of the conversation. Conditions can and do change based on things like people's moods, attitudes, and actions. Taking control of a crucial conversation requires attention to both.

Conditions that Put Safety at Risk

Participants in a crucial conversation must first know how to recognize the conditions that put the safety of the conversation at risk. The factors that indicate dangerous conditions include:

1. The moment a conversation turns from mundane to crucial. When participants fail to recognize that a conversation has become crucial, the likelihood increases that things will take a turn for the worse. Crucial conversations require different skills than mundane ones. The earlier the participants identify the importance of the conversation, the sooner they can make the necessary adjustments to their own

behavior. Some things that may indicate that a conversation has become crucial include physical symptoms such as stomach pain or a dry throat, emotional symptoms such as anger or fear, and behavioral symptoms such as pointing fingers or raised voices. Gifted communicators keep an eye on safety. They recognize when participants become fearful, or start adding harmful information to the Pool of Shared Information. A skilled observer can resist the urge to strike back when conditions become unsafe. To keep a crucial conversation on track, participants must step back and commit to creating and maintaining safety.

2. Watch out for silence and violence. The two conditions that most commonly occur in crucial conversations are silence and violence. Participants either withdraw, withholding valuable information from the other people involved, or they lash out in self-defense. Neither response creates a sense of safety.

In a safe environment, all participants feel welcome and free to add things to the Pool of Shared Information.

How to Self-Monitor

A skilled conversationalist has the ability to create safety because she knows how to monitor her own behavior and reactions. What allows her to monitor herself when others may lack the ability? She knows and understands her Style under Stress. People who fail to observe their own behavior accurately – those who are unable to monitor their own actions – usually end up resorting to silence or violence when a conversation turns crucial.

Understanding One's Style under Stress

How can a person understand his own style under stress? Asking a few key questions about his typical behavior in stressful situations can help him identify whether he usually chooses behaviors associated with silence or violence. Most people fall into one of those two categories.

Traits of a person who is silent under stress include:
- Withdrawing from conversation
- Withholding crucial information deliberately
- Avoiding stressful situations entirely
- Making jokes or using sarcasm to deflect attention or blame
- Feeling reluctant to express his true opinion

Traits of a person who is violent under stress include:
- Calling names or pointing out where others have made mistakes
- Using aggressive behavior such as finger pointing or yelling
- Making personal attacks on other participants in the conversation
- Interrupting others when they try to speak
- Moving from trying to resolve issues to trying to win the conversation

Anybody can learn how to avoid the twin traps of silence and violence by asking some tough questions about how they deal with stress and then acting to change those behaviors.

Crucial Conversations contains a detailed questionnaire that readers can use to evaluate their Style under Stress. They can then use the knowledge they gain from the quiz to refine and change the negative ways they respond to stressful situations and crucial conversations.

When a person has a deep understanding of his Style under Stress and the ability to monitor his behavior, he also has the wherewithal to do what he can to create a safe environment for the other participants in the conversation. In the absence of one person who possesses this knowledge, the chances decrease that the crucial conversation will be a successful one.

Chapter 5
Building Mutal Purpose

When a conversation turns crucial and safety goes out the window, one or more participants can rein the conversation in by creating a safe environment and building a mutual purpose. Doing so requires stepping outside of the content of the conversation, surveying the conditions, and making the necessary adjustments to create safety.

Mutual Purpose

Crucial conversations can never be successful unless the participants share a mutual purpose. If the participant has their own personal purposes, individual goals can go to war with one another, preventing a real resolution from occurring.

Creating a mutual purpose can be difficult, but a skilled conversationalist can accomplish it with some careful negotiations. First, one participant in the conversation must understand the importance of mutual purpose and know how to get all parties to agree to one.

When participants in a conversation have opposing goals, arriving at a consensus can feel impossible. To determine a mutual purpose, all participants must be willing to examine their true desires and search for common ground. The mutual purpose, once agreed upon, provides a road map for the conversation itself. For example, a wife might ask her husband to discuss their sex life. Her initial purpose involves expressing her frustration with his approach to sex, while his consists of punishing her because he feels dissatisfied. Their individual purposes lack common ground, but they can find a shared purpose: to make their sex life mutually satisfying.

Participants in a crucial conversation can identify a mutual purpose by first stepping out of the content of the conversation, and second, by searching for and agreeing upon a mutual purpose – the common ground that all parties share.

Mutual Respect

A crucial conversation can fail for many different reasons. When participants do not feel safe, or when they lack a mutual purpose, staying on track can be impossible.

Respect makes up another critical component of a crucial conversation. When mutual respect does not exist among all parties to the conversation, civility can fall by the wayside. Learning to recognize the signs that respect has eroded can be helpful:

- Emotions run high when respect leaves the room. The moment a participant feels that others do not respect her; anger and defensiveness tend to rule the day.
- Each participant must ask, "Do others feel that I

respect them?" and answer the question honestly.

- When one or more participants in the conversation has a low opinion of another participant, it proves difficult to provide the respect needed. Identifying a mutual purpose can help because it establishes common ground. When a participant feels unable to respect the whole person, he may find it possible to respect the person's goals or desires regardless. Sometimes that provides enough common ground to move the conversation forward.

Steps to Build Mutual Purpose

How can participants in a conversation create mutual respect when none appears to exist? These things may help:

1. Apologize for one's own behavior when appropriate. Everybody makes mistakes. When a person steps back from the content of the conversation and examines his own behavior, he may realize that he has made a mistake or contributed to a problem. In such a scenario, apologizing can smooth things out and restore respect.

2. Use contrast to clear up misunderstandings. Sometimes one participant in the conversation must make the effort to state clearly what he does and doesn't want. He may begin by addressing the concerns of others regarding his respect for them, and then finish by confirming his respect for them and restating his real purpose.

3. After smoothing things over, search for common ground and embrace a mutual purpose. One can

accomplish this by splitting people into groups and asking them to write down and share their goals. Often people have more common ground than they realize, and sharing can help them recognize that.

Sometimes identifying a mutual purpose requires moving beyond strategies and looking at desires instead. Many people become entrenched in a particular way of thinking, but examining desires can help people see beyond strategy.

Once the participants have successfully identified a mutual purpose, then everyone can brainstorm strategies to achieve the mutual purpose. This step ensures that everyone will feel included and can accept the strategies chosen. Having a mutual purpose can turn conflict into agreement.

Chapter 6
Stories and Dialogue

Unchecked emotion has the potential to hijack a crucial conversation about any subject. When people use their emotions to make decisions, they fail to make use of the highest-functioning parts of their brains.

How Emotions Hijack Dialogue

How can emotions hijack dialogue? Emotional people allow feelings to rule the day. They ignore logic and reason because their emotion makes it easy for them to do so. To understand why emotion can derail a crucial conversation, one must recognize the origins of emotion. Many people say things like, "She made me mad!" Statements like that place the blame on others, making the speaker seem like an innocent bystander. That view misses something important – we create our own emotions. When we fail to recognize our own role in creating emotion, we also tend to disown those emotions. When a person distances himself from emotion, she puts the blame on someone else – a condition that prohibits crucial conversations from happening.

How Feelings Drive Actions

Emotions don't exist in a vacuum. In order for them

to have the power to hijack a crucial conversation, the person who experiences those emotions must give them meaning. Something happens between the time a person experiences a particular emotion and the time she acts on it. People attach meaning to emotions by telling themselves stories to explain those emotions.

People tell themselves stories in an effort to make sense of how they feel. They assign motives to other people and make judgments about the things others do. Motives and judgments build meaning on top of emotions, and the storyteller then acts to respond to the meaning he created. In other words, the story creates the storyteller's path to action.

Mastering Stories

To prevent stories from hijacking crucial conversations, the storyteller himself must take certain steps:

1. Retrace his path. When he understands how he arrived at his emotional destination, he can do a better job of analyzing those emotions. Retracing the path includes things like looking for factual evidence that supports the story he tells himself.

2. Notice his behavior. He must identify and take responsibility for the behavior his story has inspired.

3. Get in touch with his feelings. Most human emotions have great complexity, yet people tend to oversimplify them. For example, a person may say he feels angry when the truth is that he feels violated. Using precise words can help keep oversimplification in check.

4. Analyze his stories. In the final step, the storyteller must use what he has discovered to analyze his story and separate fact from fiction.

Three Dangerous Stories

While some stories that people tell during crucial conversations are unique, some fall into specific patterns. These three dangerous stories have the potential to derail any crucial conversation:

- Victim stories. The storyteller makes herself into a hapless victim of others' follies or misbehaviors. Victim stories allow people to deflect blame and avoid responsibility.
- Villain stories. The opposite of the victim story, the villain story turns an everyday person into a hideous villain. It assigns nefarious motives and all of the blame to another party.
- Helpless stories. The storyteller who weaves a helpless story tells herself that she lacks the ability to do anything to change the situation. She may not assign blame, but neither does she make herself accountable for his situation.

These three common stories are told over and over again in countless situations. They all represent an effort to detach from the crucial conversation without having to address difficult issues or take any responsibility for what has occurred.

Create Useful Stories

Any storyteller can take a dangerous story and turn it into a useful one by using one of these simple techniques:

- Turn a victim into an actor. Instead of self-identifying as a victim, the storyteller can rewrite the tale to make herself an active participant.
- Turn a villain into a human. Instead of vilifying another person and assigning all blame to him, the storyteller can look for relatable or admirable characteristics in her opponent.
- Turn the helpless into the able. Instead of creating a passive version of herself, the storyteller can rewrite her story and cast herself as an able person with the ability to change things for the better.

Human beings love stories, but the stories they tell themselves to avoid crucial conversations can be harmful and counterproductive. Mastering the story can rescue a crucial conversation and make it productive.

Chapter 7
Speaking Persuasively

Every crucial conversation requires the introduction of risky information into the Pool of Shared Meaning. Safe information creates little drama or risk. The introduction of risky information has the potential to turn a normal conversation into a crucial one very quickly.

Introduce Risky Information

When it becomes necessary to introduce risky information into the Pool of Shared Information, it requires finesse. A skilled conversationalist uses the following steps when doing so:

- He expresses himself with confidence. He believes that he deserves to be heard and he presents it in a way that makes that clear.
- He expresses himself with humility. That might seem contradictory, but many people confused confidence with arrogance. A skilled conversationalist can project confidence in a way that respects the other people in the conversation.
- He expresses himself with honesty. He finds a way to convey sensitive information without being hurtful or unkind – but he doesn't hold back, either.

- He expresses himself with skill. He understands that candor and safety can go hand in hand, and he has the ability to express the truth in a way that maintains safety.

STATE Your Path

The above traits might present a challenge, but the possibility exists that one can exemplify all of them by using the STATE method of introducing risky information:

1. SHARE the facts. A skilled conversationalist remembers that the facts are the basis of her story and she always starts with them.

2. TELL the story. She then takes a moment to tell the story she wrote to the other participants in the conversation. Without the story, the facts may not be controversial. They story provides context for the facts.

3. ASK for others' paths. She follows her story with a question, asking the other participants in the conversation to share their own paths. Their paths may include facts, opinions, and stories.

4. TALK tentatively. She softens her language by saying things like "I'm starting to wonder if..." or "Is it possible that..." These words allow room for conversation because they leave space for disagreement and differences of opinion.

5. ENCOURAGE testing. A skilled conversationalist finally requests opposing opinions and encourages debate. When everyone in the conversation feels that his or her opinions are valued, the likelihood

increases that the crucial conversation will have a successful conclusion.

The What Skills

The first three steps in the STATE method represent "what" skills – in other words, what a conversationalist needs to do to introduce risky information.

1. Sharing facts means starting with the least controversial information available. Rather than accusing a co-worker of embezzlement, for example, a skilled conversationalist might begin the STATE method by saying something like, "I found a few discrepancies in the books and I'm hoping you can help me clear them up."

2. Telling his story means that the person who initiated the conversation might say, "I don't want to believe this, but the conclusion I have drawn is that someone has been taking money out of our account without permission."

3. Asking for the other person's path creates an environment of safety by making him feel that his opinion matters. Continuing with the embezzlement example, a way to ask for the path might involve saying, "Can you tell me what you think about these numbers?"

The first three steps all involve WHAT a person must do to introduce risky information to the pool.

The HOW Skills

The final two steps in the STATE method have to do with

how a person introduces risky information:

4. Talking tentatively means that the person who started the conversation must present his story as a story and not as fact. Using the above example, he might say, "You are the only other person who has access to this account, and that makes me think that you might be responsible. I'm hoping that I'm wrong about that." A statement like this one stops short of making an outright accusation, and it may help the other person feel safe.

5. The final step in STATE requires encouraging testing. One way to do that might be following up the above statement with a question. "Do you have an alternative explanation for the discrepancy?" This simple question encourages the other person to share opinions and facts that might differ from the questioner's conclusion.

The STATE method provides an easy way to introduce risky information and defuse emotion, making it possible to keep a conversation on track.

Chapter 8
Listening Skills

After using the STATE method to introduce risky information, the person who started the crucial conversation must employ a few key listening skills to avoid stalling the conversation.

How to Listen to Others' Paths

Encouraging others to share their paths only works if the person who did the encouraging has the ability to listen well. These four simple tips can help:

- Be sincere. The participants in a conversation can sense it if the person who asked about their path lacks sincerity. A skilled conversationalist asks and sincerely wants to hear the answer.
- Be curious. Not every person asked to share his path will be willing. Curiosity, in the form of careful questions, can help provide the necessary encouragement.
- Stay curious. Sometimes it requires patience and persistence to get a person to share his entire path. A skilled person understands this and asks follow-up questions to keep things on track.
- Be patient. As a person shares her path, she may

become emotional or argumentative. The temptation to jump in and defend oneself may be strong, but remaining silent and calm will allow the whole story to come out.

In other words, asking questions to encourage sharing can be helpful, but interrupting or displaying a lack of interest can destroy a crucial conversation quickly.

Getting Others to Tell Their Stories

Sometimes sincerity, curiosity, and patience may not provide sufficient incentive for a person to share his story. These things can help:

1. Trace the origins of the story. When a person tries to articulate her story, she may provide incomplete information. Asking questions to get to the heart of what she's saying can help clarify.

2. Break the cycle. Instead of joining in a story that includes blame and recriminations, a skilled conversationalist has the ability to break the cycle by asking questions and listening instead of trying to defend herself and continuing the cycle of destruction.

The acronym AMPP can provide some guidance to help persuade sharing. The authors refer to these as power listening tools:

*   ASK questions to get things going. The question can be simple. For example, "What's going on?" or "Can you tell me your opinion?" may be enough to get the ball rolling.

- Mirror the other person's emotions. Using phrases such as "It seems to me that you're feeling undervalued" can help make the person who shares his story feel understood and heard.
- Paraphrase the story back to the person who told it. Not every participant in a crucial conversation will do a good job telling his story. Instead of making assumptions that can lead to further misunderstanding, a skilled person paraphrases the story back to the teller in his own word to make sure that he understands it.
- Prime the pump. When a person expresses reluctance to share, someone may have to take a leap and make an educated guess about what he thinks. For example, "Is the reason you feel that way because you think that we're only interested in the bottom line?" A question like this opens up discussion because it offers a safe path for people to express opinions.

Understand the Other Person's Path to Action

Both STATE and AMPP provide people with the skills they need to understand another person's path to action. When a person in a conversation starts using aggressive language and behavior, understanding is crucial. That person didn't arrive at an aggressive place without some effort and storytelling of his own. The only way to grasp it requires using the tools provided to follow them down their path to action and understand how they arrived at their destination.

Follow the ABCs

The final listening skill that can help resolve a crucial conversation involves following three simple steps, which the authors refer to as the ABCs:

- Agree. A lot of disagreements arise from very small things, but when emotions run high, the participants can end up making mountains out of molehills. A skilled conversationalist recognizes points of agreement and concedes them so that agreements don't turn into arguments.

- Build. After finding a place of agreement, the next step involves building upon it. For example, the person who started the agreement might say, "Another thing I think we agree on..." or "Absolutely, and I'd just like to add that...." Statements like these add information and build on agreement. The more agreement that exists, the less likely it becomes that arguments will flare up.

- Compare. After building agreements, the final step involves comparing the differences that exist between the parties. This might involve using the STATE method to describe one's path.

The importance of listening as an essential part of any crucial conversation cannot be understated.

Chapter 9
Turning Conversations Into Action

Crucial Conversations focuses on encouraging the free flow of information between the involved parties for a very simple reason – information and understanding provide the basis for the goal of any crucial conversation. Talk only takes people so far. For a crucial conversation to be truly successful, it must lead to "smart, unified, and committed actions."

Moving Dialogue to Decisions

Even when information flows freely, arriving at a decision at the conclusion of a crucial conversation can pose come challenges. Dialogue forms an essential part of a crucial conversation, but it differs from a decision. Part of the issue involves deciding who has the power to decide.

- When a clear line of authority exists, the person in charge makes the final decision. For example, a parent sets the rules for his children.
- When no clear line of authority exists, the decision becomes a bit tricky. The participants must negotiate to decide how to decide.

Negotiating a decision-making process might not seem easy, but it can help to know which possibilities exist.

Four Methods of Decision Making

Deciding how to decide involves choosing amount four basic options:

- A command decision arises either from a person with clear authority, or from circumstances that do not allow for dissent. For example, a decision about product pricing might occur as the result of a competitor slashing prices or customers demanding lower prices. A command decision requires the people affected to do the best they can under the circumstances because it may not like a decision in the traditional sense of the word.

- A consulted decision happens when the ultimate decision-maker invites opinions, suggestions, and comments before making her decision. She has the final say, but she wants other people to feel that their input has been heard.

- A voted decision requires all of the participants in the conversation to cast a vote for the resolution they prefer. This method of decision-making might pose some problems, but sometimes "majority rules" can lead the way out of a tricky situation.

- A consensus decision requires everyone involved agreeing on the same course of action. It can lead to high quality decisions – or to a massive waste of time.

To decide which decision-making method to use, it may help to ask some simple questions:

- Who genuinely cares about the decision?
- Who has crucial information required to make the decision?
- Who needs to agree on the decision?
- How many people need to be involved?

For example, if only a few people involved in the conversation have crucial information, the best option might involve letting them decide.

Making Assignments

Once the relevant parties come to a decision, the next step involves translating that decision into concrete action. This requires concrete steps to eliminate confusion. Resolve the following:

- Who? All essential tasks must be assigned to a specific person. No task should be assigned to the group as a whole or left unassigned.
- Does what? Spell out the precise specifications of what needs to be done and when it must be completed. Breaking work up into small pieces provides an easy way to track progress.
- By when? Deadlines help prevent confusion and misunderstanding. Instead of telling an employee that a job must be done by next week, tell him that it must be done by Friday at three o'clock. That eliminates the possibility of miscommunication.
- How and when will follow-ups occur? This step requires setting boundaries and expectations. Holding people accountable might be uncomfortable for some, but it can save future

trouble. For example, an office manager might assign a research project to an employee and say, "You have until 5:00 on Monday to finish your research. Please email it to me when you're done with it, and then we'll sit down and talk about the next step." Setting clear-cut expectations for follow-ups makes it easy for employees and colleagues to manage their time.

- Document work. The final step involves careful documentation of decisions, work assignments, deadlines, and follow-ups. Documentation provides a clear framework for holding people accountable for what they have agreed to do. It ensures that the entire team understands what must be completed and when. Skipping the documentation step has the potential to create problems down the line. As such, documentation forms an important component of any crucial conversation, whether it happens in the workplace or at home.

When a crucial conversation ends with a strong decision and carefully articulated assignments, it accomplishes several things. It resolves the issue that led to the crucial conversation in the first place, and it helps lay the groundwork for successful resolution of future crucial conversations.

Chapter 10
Conclusion

For people who lack the skills to navigate critical conversations, the introduction of risky or controversial topics can feel like a minefield. *Crucial Conversations* provides a set of clearly defined and explained tools that make it possible for anybody, in a professional or personal setting, to do the following:

- Identify crucial conversations by recognizing the three things that turn a mundane conversation into a crucial one: different opinions, strong emotions, and high stakes.
- Understand the issues that complicate conversations, such as the "fight or flight" response, lack of preparation, and lack of practice.
- Refuse the Fool's Choice and recognize the possibility of discussing tricky topics without creating enemies.
- Contribute to the Pool of Shared Meaning in a helpful and respectful way.
- Start with heart by identifying the true goals and refocusing the brain on the important things in the conversation.
- Clarify the desired outcome by looking for 'And.'

- Recognize when safety is at risk.
- Self-monitor to identify one's Style under Stress.
- Create safety by avoiding silence and violence.
- Understand what it means to have a mutual purpose.
- Find a way to create mutual respect among all parties.
- Use simple tools to find or create a mutual purpose for all participants in the conversation.
- Understand how stories can hijack dialogue.
- Analyze your own story and emotions.
- Identify three dangerous stories, the Victim Story, the Villain Story, and the Helpless Story, and rewrite them as useful stories.
- Introduce risky facts into the Pool of Shared Information.
- STATE your path (Share your facts, Tell your story, Ask for others' paths, Talk tentatively, and Encourage Sharing.)
- Listen to others' stories with curiosity and patience.
- Use AMPP (Ask, Mirror, Paraphrase, Prime) to encourage others to tell their stories.
- Follow the ABCs to resolve disagreements (Agree, Build, Compare.)
- Understand the four methods of decision-making and choose the best one.
- Turn dialogue into action by assigning tasks, setting deadlines, and clarifying expectations.
- Documenting decisions and assignments to avoid future confusion.

- Specify the procedure for following up on assigned tasks.

The techniques described in Crucial Conversations can help people navigate difficult and risk conversation in any area of life, whether it is in a personal relationship, at school, or in the workplace.

Book Summary of *Crucial Conversations* by Kerry Patterson, Joseph Grenny, Ron McMillan, and Al Switzler

Executive Reads

Crucial Conversations

What Makes a Crucial Conversation?

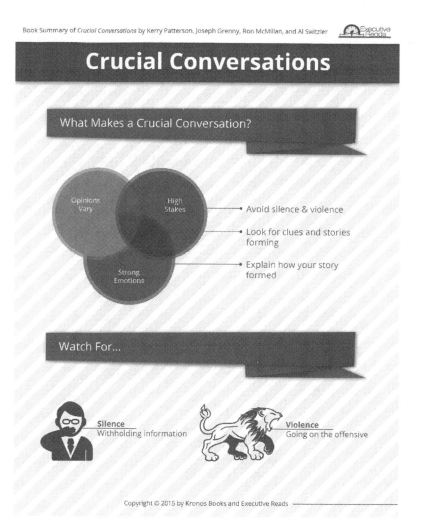

- Opinions Vary
- High Stakes
- Strong Emotions

→ Avoid silence & violence

→ Look for clues and stories forming

→ Explain how your story formed

Watch For...

Silence
Withholding information

Violence
Going on the offensive

Crucial Conversations

Book Summary of *Crucial Conversations* by Kerry Patterson, Joseph Grenny, Ron McMillan, and Al Switzler

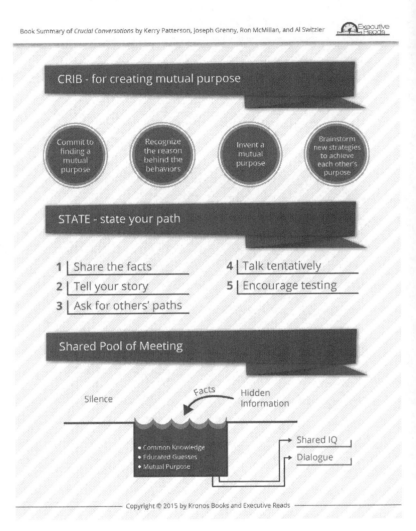

CRIB - for creating mutual purpose

Commit to finding a mutual purpose

Recognize the reason behind the behaviors

Invent a mutual purpose

Brainstorm new strategies to achieve each other's purpose

STATE - state your path

1 | Share the facts
2 | Tell your story
3 | Ask for others' paths
4 | Talk tentatively
5 | Encourage testing

Shared Pool of Meeting

Silence   Facts   Hidden Information

- Common Knowledge
- Educated Guesses
- Mutual Purpose

Shared IQ
Dialogue

Thank you for reading the Executive Reads summary of *Crucial Conversations*.

For your convenience we provide a full-color downloadable PDF of the crib sheet infographic.

http://www.executivereads.com/infographics/Crucial_Conversations_2334C.pdf

To keep up-to-date with Executive Reads news, releases, freebies, or business article summaries (you choose), subscribe to our newsletter:

http://www.executivereads.com/newsletter

We never share your information with anybody.

If you have feedback, good or bad, we'd love to hear from you at: feedback@executivereads.com.

Thank you.

Made in the USA
San Bernardino, CA
23 March 2020